Cornerstones

# Out on the Playground

Carolyn Farr          Jane Hutchison

Carol McGrail         Carol Pawlowski

Featured Illustrator: Michael Martchenko

gagelearning

**Project Management and Editorial**: First Folio Resource Group, Inc.
Supervising Editor: Fran Cohen
Copy Editor: Jane McWhinney
Production Editor: Francine Geraci

**Gage Editorial**
Joe Banel
Darleen Rotozinski

**Gage Production**
Anna Kress
Bev Crann

**Design, Art Direction & Electronic Assembly**
Pronk&Associates/David Montle

**Acknowledgments**
Every reasonable effort has been made to trace ownership of copyrighted material. Information that would enable the publisher to correct any reference or credit in future editions would be appreciated.

We acknowledge the financial support of the Government of Canada through the Book Publishing Industry Development Program for our publishing activities.

**Photo Credits**
6-7 Dave Starrett; 28 G.I. Bernard/Animals Animals; 28-31 (Ant border) Raymond A. Mendez/Animals Animals; 29 above Raymond A. Mendez/Animals Animals, below Richard La Val; 30 Bill Ivy; 31 Raymond A. Mendez/Animals Animals; 32 Tim Flach/Tony Stone Images.

**Illustrations**
6-7 Bill Suddick; 4-5, 8-11, 27 Michael Martchenko; 12-17 Bernadette Lau; 18-26 Bryan Stewart.

**Canadian Cataloguing in Publication Data**

Main entry under title:

Gage cornerstones : out on the playground

ISBN 0-7715-1234-1

1. Student books (Primary). I. Farr, Carolyn, et al. II. Title: Cornerstones: out on the playground. III. Title: Out on the Playground.

PE1119.G23 1999          428.6          C99-931150-6

**Advisory Team**
Jane Abernethy, Chipman & Fredericton SD, NB

Gwen Bartnik, Vancouver SB, BC

Susan Boehnke, Durham DSB, ON

Lisa Bond, Catholic Independent Schools of Vancouver Archdiocese, BC

Marg Craig, Lambton-Kent DSB, ON

Sheila Devine Ross, Southwest Regional SB, NS

Laurel Galt, Durham DSB, ON

Gloria Gustafson, Coquitlam DSB, BC

Lise Hawkins, Toronto DSB, ON

Sharon Kinakin, Langley SD #35, BC

Jane Koberstein, Mission DSB, BC

Irene Kovats, Calgary CSSB, AB

Rosemary Lloyd, Durham DSB, ON

Martin MacDonald, Strait Regional SB, NS

Sharon Morris, Toronto CDSB, ON

Cheryl Norman, Delta SD #37, BC

Jennifer Pinches, Calgary CSD, AB

Joanne Pizzuto, Windsor DSB, ON

Pearl Reimer, Edmonton PSB, AB

Maureen Rodniski, Winnipeg SD, MB

Patricia Rooney, Wellington County CDSB, ON

Barbara Rushton, Annapolis Valley Regional SB, NS

Lynn Strangway, Simcoe DSB, ON

Anna Totten, Toronto CDSB, ON

Doreen M. Valverde, Southwest Regional SB, NS

Suzanne Witkin, Toronto DSB, ON

ISBN 0-7715-1234-1
4 5 6 GG 03 02
Printed and bound in Canada.

# Table of Contents

All selections by Carolyn Farr, Jane Hutchison, Carol McGrail, and Carol Pawlowski.

4

# Out on the Playground

Out on the playground
What do we see?
Ants and bugs
And birds in a tree.

Out on the playground
What do we hear?
A happy laugh
And a great big cheer!

Out on the playground
What do we do?
We run, we skip,
And we shout, "Yahoo!"

# Look!

Wow!

Look.

Look at all the ants!

# Ants

Ants, ants

13

Can you see the ants?

big ants

small ants

ants, ants, ants

# Ants, Ants

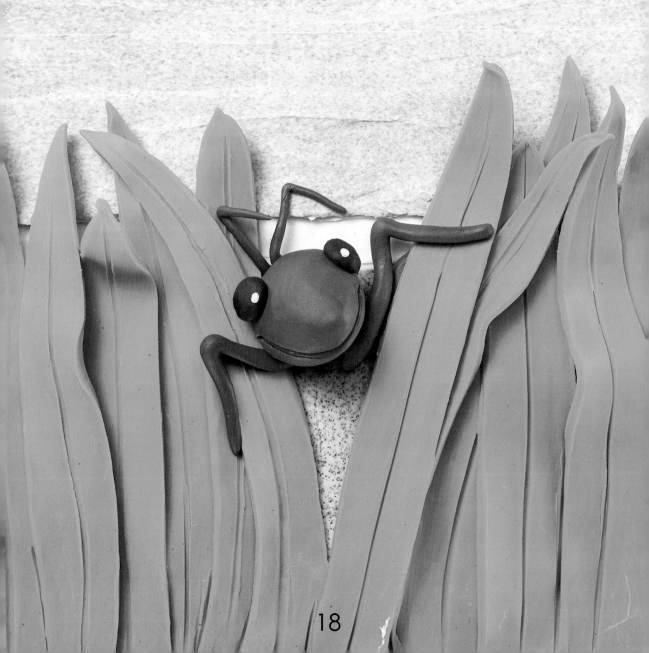

Look on the sidewalk.

Look on the wall.

Look on the green grass,
ants big and small.

# No Ants

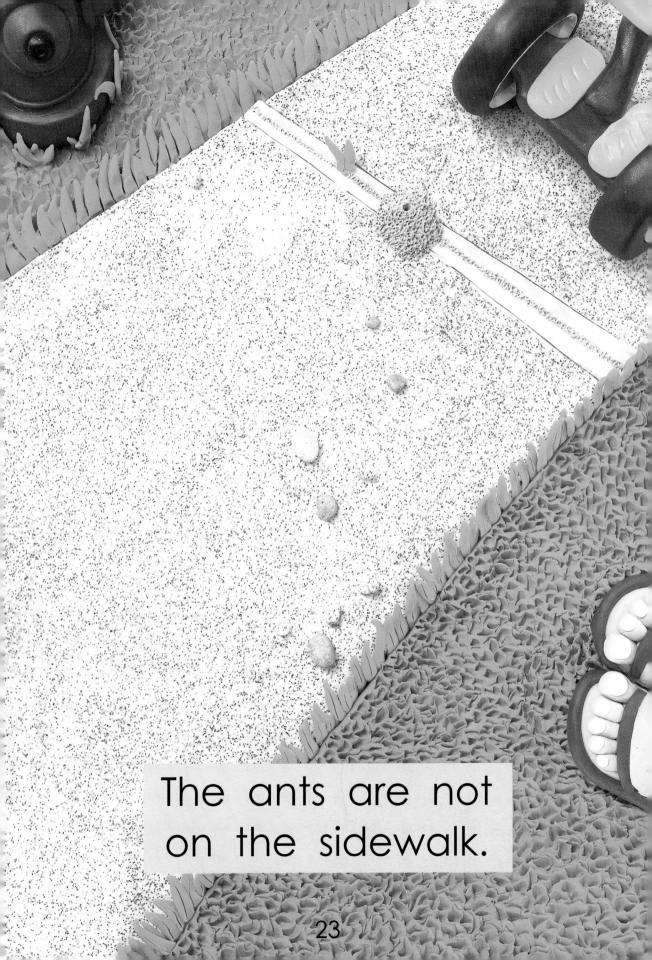

The ants are not
on the sidewalk.

The ants are not
on the wall.

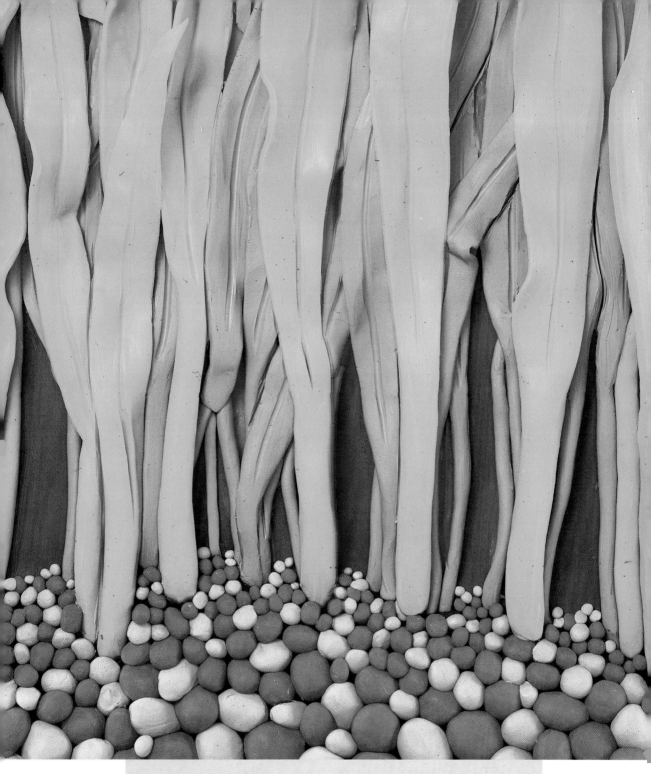

The ants are not
on the green grass.

The ants are not
here at all.

# The Ant Book

Look. Here is a book
on ants.

# Awesome Ants

Here is a red ant.

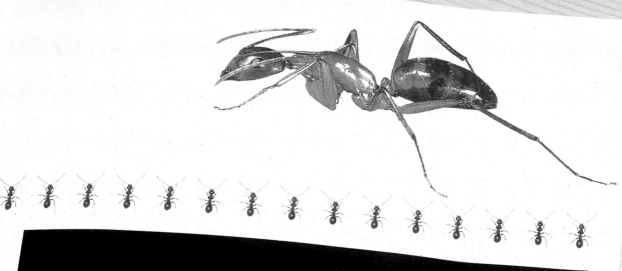

Here is a brown ant.

Here is a black ant.

Here is a queen ant.

Ants are awesome.